The Three Billy Goats Gruff

Retold by Laurel Dickey
Illustrations by Tracy La Rue Hohn

Pioneer Valley Educational Press, Inc.

"I'm hungry," said the little Billy Goat Gruff.

"I'm hungry," said the middle Billy Goat Gruff.

"I'm hungry, too," said the big Billy Goat Gruff.

3

The little Billy Goat Gruff
went over the bridge.
Trip-trap, trip-trap, trip-trap.

"Who's that going over my bridge?" said the troll. "I will eat you up!"

"No, no," said the little Billy Goat Gruff. "My brother is coming over the bridge, too. He's bigger. Eat him up!"

The middle Billy Goat Gruff went over the bridge. Trip-trap, trip-trap, trip-trap.

"Who's that going over my bridge?" said the troll. "I will eat you up!"

"No, no," said the middle Billy Goat Gruff. "My brother is coming over the bridge, too. He's bigger. Eat him up!"

The big Billy Goat Gruff
went over the bridge.
Trip-trap, trip-trap, trip-trap.

"Who's that going over my bridge?" said the troll. "I will eat you up!"

"No you will not!"
said the
big Billy Goat Gruff.
"Oh, no you will not!"

14